FIGHTING A FIRE

BRENDA WILLIAMS
ILLUSTRATED BY ANDREW MACDONALD

Kingfisher Books

Advisers: Mary Jane Drummond, Tutor in Primary Education, Cambridge Institute of Education, Cambridge
Iris Walkinshaw, Headteacher, Rushmore Infants School, Hackney, London
Patricia Brown, Children's Librarian North Kensington Library, London

Technical advisers: Divisional Officer Jack Frost and Station Officer Brian Clark, London Fire Brigade

The author and editor would also like to thank the firefighters at the London Fire HQ, Lambeth and at Homerton Fire Station, and the Gloucestershire Fire and Rescue Service

Photographs: Gloucestershire Fire and Rescue Service 10; Zefa 11 *top*, London Fire Brigade Photographic Services 11 *bottom*

First published in 1987 by Kingfisher Books Limited, Elsley House, 24–30 Great Titchfield Street, London W1P 7AD
A Grisewood & Dempsey Company.

Reprinted 1987

BRITISH CATALOGUING IN PUBLICATION DATA
Williams, Brenda
Fighting a fire—(Stepping stones 4, 5, 6)
1. Fire extinction—Juvenile literature
I. Title   II. Macdonald, Andrew III. Series
628.9′25   TH9148
ISBN: 0 86272 250 0

Edited by Vanessa Clarke
Designed by Nicholas Cannan
Illustration research by Penny Warn
Cover designed by Pinpoint Design Company
Phototypeset by Southern Positives and Negatives
(SPAN), Lingfield, Surrey
Printed in Spain.

Contents

This is the fire station and these are the people who work at the fire station. They are called firefighters. They put out fires and protect people from fire.

Firefighters have to be ready to fight fires at any time, day or night, so they take it in turns to work at the fire station. The station has a dormitory with beds where the firefighters rest at night.

A Station Officer is in charge of the firefighters with a Sub-Officer to help. Paul, Liz and Andy are at the station today. Their Sub-Officer is Bill.

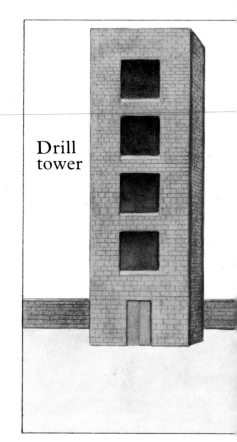

Drill tower

Station Officer, Brian   Sub-Officer, Bill   Liz   Paul

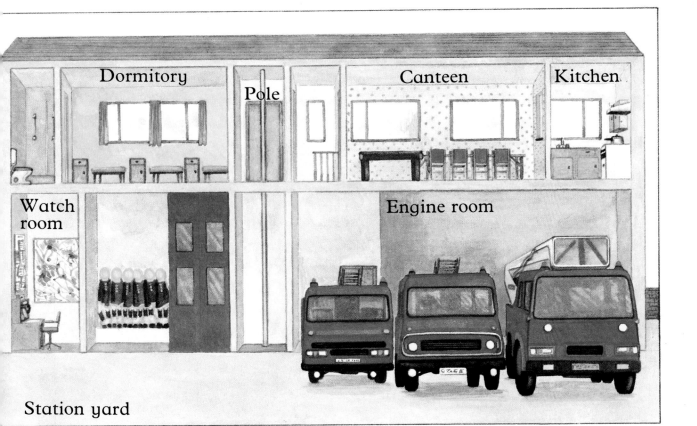

Dormitory

Pole

Canteen

Kitchen

Watch room

Engine room

Station yard

Kevin   Sam   Jack   Leo   Joe   Dusty   Andy

We are some of the firefighters of the Red Watch.

5

The fire station has three engines. Bill, Liz, Paul and Andy are the crew on the pump engine. This engine carries 1,136 litres of water, 350 metres of hose, two short ladders and one long extending ladder, rescue equipment and a pump. The pump is the most important part of this fire engine because it forces water out through the hoses to fight the fire.

Siren

Lights

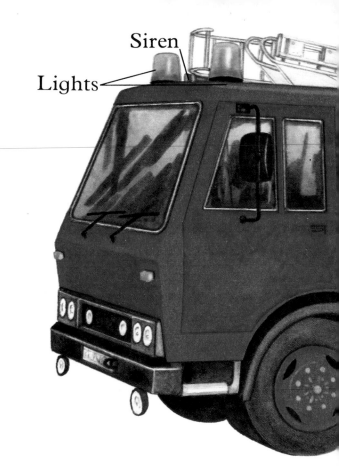

Here are some other kinds of engines:

The Hydraulic Platform (HP) Engine carries firefighters up and down the outside of tall buildings. You can see it working on pages 24 and 26.

The Turntable Ladder Engine is used for rescuing people. It does not carry water or hoses.

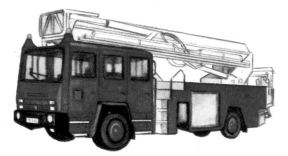

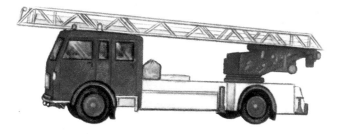

Hoses

Saw, yes, first aid kit, yes, breathing apparatus, yes.. but where's the axe?

Pump

The Rescue Tender carries extra rescue equipment to any emergency.

The Foam Tender carries foam, not water. It is used to fight chemical and oil fires at factories, airports and on motorways.

When there are no fires, the firefighters practise their fire drill. There is a drill tower in the station yard and the firefighters pretend it is a burning building. Andy practises rescuing a dummy person made of some old clothes stuffed with hoses.

Putting up the extending ladder

The firefighter pulls the rope to make the ladder go up. The other firefighters hold the heavy ladder steady.

This isn't a real person but it is just as heavy!

Paul is showing a new firefighter how to hold the hose. The hose is fixed to the pump engine. Another hose goes from the pump engine to a hydrant and the hydrant leads to water-pipes under the ground. The pump draws up water through the hose on the hydrant and shoots it out of Paul's hose.

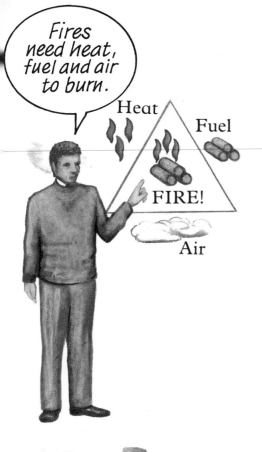

Fires need heat, fuel and air to burn.

Heat

Fuel

FIRE!

Air

Firefighters hose water onto most fires to cool them down and stop air getting to the flames. The fire goes out because fire needs heat and air to burn.

But water is dangerous to use on oil and chemical fires because it can make them spread. Firefighters spray thick foam or powder on these fires instead of water. The fire goes out because air cannot reach it.

Firefighters cannot put out forest fires with water because forest fires are too big. Instead they try to stop the flames spreading. They cut down trees and use

House fire

We fight fires in homes with water.

Forest fire

I beat out sparks that jump across the path in front of a forest fire.

excavators to dig out earth and make a wide path in front of the fire. When the fire reaches the path it stops because there is nothing more to burn.

We wear protective suits if there are dangerous chemicals around.

Oil fire

Firefighters eat their meals at the fire station when they are at work. Today, just as the Red Watch are sitting down to dinner, the emergency bells ring. Lights flash. Everyone rushes to the engine room. The firefighters slide down the shiny pole because it is faster than running down the stairs.

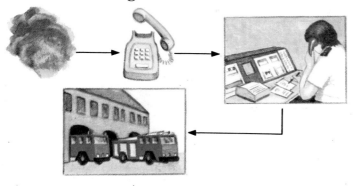

"Where's the fire?" Bill runs to the watch room to find out. He picks up the message which tells where the fire is. Then he jumps into the pump engine with the rest of the crew.

The station bells stop after 30 seconds. By then the fire engines are on their way to the fire.

The firefighters kick off their shoes as they run to the engine. They get dressed in their fire gear while it rushes along the road.

First they put on their scarves and hard hats. Then they pull on heavy rubber boots and waterproof trousers. The trousers will not burn because they are made of fire-resisting plastic.

Putting on the scarf   the boots   the trousers

They put on tunics made of wool. The wool soaks up water when the firefighters use the hoses and so does not burn easily.

Last of all, the firefighters strap themselves into the breathing apparatus which is clipped to the seats. When they reach the fire, they press a lever and jump out with the breathing apparatus on their backs.

We will need our breathing apparatus if there is thick smoke.

the tunic

the breathing apparatus

16

"Where's the fire?" asks Andy in the pump engine. "In a shop in the High Street," says Paul. "We'll need to find water fast. This map shows two hydrants we can use for our hoses."

Close behind the pump engine comes the HP engine. The sirens are blaring and the blue lights are flashing. Traffic moves out of the way to let them pass.

18

The fire at the shop is burning fiercely. The crew jump out and get to work. Andy runs to the hydrant and lifts the lid. Paul throws him the hose and Andy fixes it to the hydrant. Liz turns on the pump.
Soon the firefighters begin spraying water at the building.

I hope there's no one left inside.

People are hurrying away from the thick smoke and heat. Some are already in the street. Others are coming down the fire escape.

The most important job at a fire is rescuing people. Bill tells his crew to go inside to look for people left behind. Paul, Liz and Andy pull on the masks of their breathing apparatus. They breathe air from the cylinders on their backs. Without the breathing apparatus they would stifle in thick smoke.

Bill counts the firefighters as they go in and come out.

Inside the building it is hot and smoky. Paul twists the nozzle on the hose to make it spray out a huge circle of water.

The spray pushes back the smoke and the heat. It makes a shield of water and the firefighters walk behind it up the stairs.

21

The firefighters open a door to the furniture
department on the second floor. The fire is
hottest here and the smoke and heat knock
them back. Paul signals to the others,
"Let's look in those rooms over there."
The firefighters start to search the rooms.

In one room they find two people. Liz makes them crouch down near the floor where there is less smoke. Now they can breathe better. Paul looks down into the street to see if the firefighters outside have seen them.

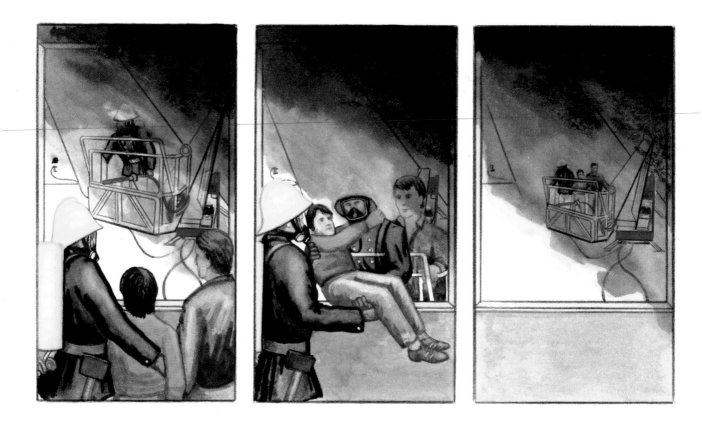

The cage at the end of the HP ladder comes
up towards them. A firefighter in the cage
guides it close to the window and Andy
helps the trapped people to climb out of the
window and into the cage.

When the people are safely inside, the
firefighter uses the control in the cage to
lower it to the ground.

Paul, Liz and Andy search all the rooms on the second and third floors. There is nobody left inside.

"Let's go," signals Paul. But on the way out Liz hears a noise. It is a dog barking. They follow the noise and find a dog with its owner. She has hurt her leg trying to escape and her dog has stayed with her, barking for help.

Andy carries the woman outside to an ambulance and Liz takes the dog. Three pump engines are fighting the fire now and the flames are dying. High above the street, two firefighters on the HP ladder are spraying water through the windows.

More firefighters are inside the building with their hoses. Sub-Officer Bill is talking about the fire to a radio reporter.

Everyone's safe and the fire is under control.

The flames are out now. Everybody is safe. But Paul, Liz and Andy go back inside the building. The firefighters must go on spraying water onto the smoking ashes to cool them down. Hot ashes can start another fire.

Investigators from the Fire Investigation Unit search the burnt building. They take photographs of the damage and collect pieces of burnt wood from the furniture department. They hope to find out what started the fire from these clues.

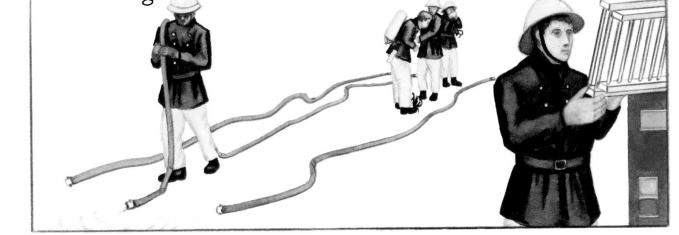

At last it is time for the firefighters to pack up the hoses and hoist the ladders onto the engines. One by one the engines leave.
The fire is over.

29

All the firefighters are tired and hungry. But before they can rest they have more work to do. They have to clean the engine straightaway to make it ready for the next fire call.

Liz takes the breathing apparatus to be cleaned, refilled and tested. Paul scrubs the sooty hoses and Andy starts to clean the engine. They make sure that the clean equipment is put back inside the fire engine. Now the crew can go to the canteen.

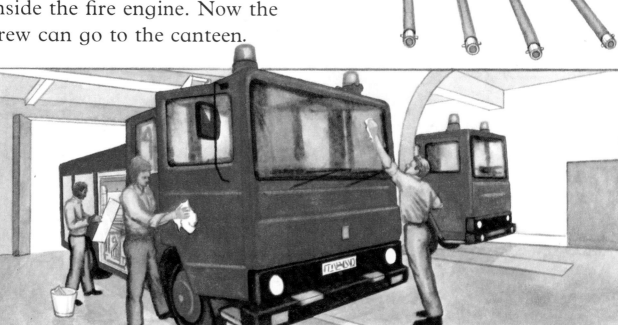

The Sub-Officer has to write a report on the fire. He writes down what the firefighters did to put it out. Then he goes to the canteen too.

Perhaps the Red Watch will be able to finish their meal this time. Whatever happens, the firefighters are ready. The fire gear is ready and the engines are ready to go out and fight the next fire.

31

Index

The fire call

How the message arrives at the station:

1 The fire has started

2 Someone calls 999 and speaks to the operator

3 The Officer in the Fire Control Centre

1

2

3 uses maps and computers to find the nearest fire station and sends it a message by teleprinter machine.

4 The teleprinter machine at the fire station types out a message saying where the fire is.